Poetry for Students, Volume 4

Staff

Series Editor: Mary Ruby.

Contributing Editors: Margaret Haerens and Lynn Koch.

Managing Editor: Drew Kalasky.

Research: Victoria B. Cariappa, *Research Team Manager.* Andy Malonis, *Research Specialist.* Julia C. Daniel, Tamara C. Nott, Tracie A. Richardson, and Cheryl L. Warnock, *Research Associates.* Jeffrey Daniels, *Research Assistant.*

Permissions: Susan M. Trosky, *Permissions Manager.* Kimberly F. Smilay, *Permissions Specialist.* Kelly Quin, *Permissions Assistant.*

Production: Mary Beth Trimper, *Production Director.* Evi Seoud, *Assistant Production Manager.* Shanna Heilveil, *Production Assistant.*

Graphic Services: Randy Bassett, *Image Database*

Supervisor. Robert Duncan and Michael Logusz, *Imaging Specialists.* Pamela A. Reed, *Photography Coordinator.* Gary Leach, *Macintosh Artist.*

Product Design: Cynthia Baldwin, *Product Design Manager.* Cover Design: Michelle DiMercurio, *Art Director.* Page Design: Pamela A. E. Galbreath, *Senior Art Director.*

coordination, expression, arrangement, and classification of the information. All rights to this publication will be vigorously defended.

Copyright © 1999
Gale Research
27500 Drake Rd.
Farmington Hills, MI 48331-3535

ISBN 0-7876-2725-9
ISSN 1094-7019

Printed in the United States of America.
10 9 8 7 6 5 4 3 2 1

The Rime of the Ancient Mariner

Samuel Taylor Coleridge

1798

Introduction

"The Rime of the Ancient Mariner" is the first poem in *Lyrical Ballads,* the collaborative effort of Samuel Taylor Coleridge and William Wordsworth designed to explore new directions in poetic language and style, and move away from the formal and highly stylized literature of the eighteenth century. This collection is considered by many critics to be the first expression of what has come to be the Romantic movement in English poetry. Coleridge's contribution, "The Rime of the Ancient

Mariner," was written in imitation of the form, language, and style of earlier ballads, but it embodied Romantic characteristics with its use of supernatural and Gothic imagery. The first publication of the poem in 1798 was received with little enthusiasm. Several critics objected to Coleridge's misuse of Old English, and (Wordsworth included) the over-extravagance of his supernatural imagery. Subsequently Coleridge, for the 1800 edition of the work, eliminated many Gothic elements and antiquated words. However, in an 1817 edition of his collected poems, *Sybilline Leaves,* Coleridge replaced some of the language he had previously deleted. Since the plot and theme had been considered confusing, he also included a marginal gloss, or set of notes, explaining the action of the poem. This is the version of "The Rime of the Ancient Mariner" that currently appears in most anthologies and textbooks.

On its simplest level, "The Rime of the Ancient Mariner" is a tale of crime, punishment, and redemption: a Mariner shoots an albatross (a bird of good fortune) and is gravely punished by an extraneous force for this act. By learning to love, however, the Mariner partially redeems himself: for his penance he must wander the earth and retell his tale, explaining to people he encounters the lessons he has learned. Beyond this basic level of comprehension, critics seldom agree on a standard interpretation of the poem. With the richness and variety of the imagery, the complexity of the symbols, and the multiple levels of meaning, "The Rime of the Ancient Mariner" still retains its magic for the reader.

Coleridge was born in 1772 in the town of Ottery St. Mary, Devon, England, the tenth child of John Coleridge, a minister and schoolmaster, and his wife, Ann Bowdon Coleridge. Coleridge was a dreamy, isolative child and read constantly. At the age of ten his father died and he was sent to Christ's Hospital, a boarding school in London where he was befriended by fellow student Charles Lamb. In 1791 he entered Cambridge University, showing promise as a gifted writer and brilliant conversationalist. He studied to become a minister, but in 1794, before completing his degree, Coleridge left Cambridge. He went on a walking tour to Oxford where he became friends with poet Robert Southey. Inspired by the initial events of the French Revolution, Coleridge and Southey collaborated on *The Fall of Robespierre. An Historic Drama* (1794). As an outgrowth of their shared belief in liberty and equality for everyone, they developed a plan for "pantisocracy," an egalitarian and self-sufficient agricultural system to be built in Pennsylvania. The pantisocratic philosophy required every member to be married, and at Southey's urging, Coleridge wed Sarah Fricker, the sister of Southey's fiancee. However, the match proved disastrous and Coleridge's unhappy marriage was a source of grief to him throughout his life. To compound these difficulties, Southey later lost interest in the scheme, abandoning it in 1795.

Coleridge then moved to Nether Stowey in England's West Country. Lamb, William Hazlitt, and other writers visited him there, making up an informal literary community. In 1796 William Wordsworth, with whom Coleridge had exchanged letters for some years, moved into the area. The two poets became instant friends, and they began a literary collaboration. Around this time Coleridge composed "Kubla Khan" and the first version of "Rime of the Ancient Mariner"; the latter work was included as the opening poem in Coleridge and Wordsworth's joint effort, *Lyrical Ballads, with a few Other Poems,* which was published in 1798. That same year, Coleridge traveled to Germany where he developed an interest in the German philosophers Immanuel Kant, Friedrich von Schelling, and the brothers Friedrich and August Wilhelm von Schlegel; he later introduced German aesthetic theory in England through his critical writing. Soon after his return in 1799, Coleridge settled in Keswick near the Lake District, which now gained for him—together with Wordsworth and Southey who had also moved to the area—the title "Lake Poet." During this period, Coleridge suffered poor health and personal strife; his marriage was failing and he had fallen in love with Wordsworth's sister-in-law, Sarah Hutchinson—a love that was unrequited and a source of great pain. He began taking opium as a remedy for his poor health.

Seeking a more temperate climate and to

improve his morale, Coleridge began a two-year trip to Italy, Sicily, and Malta in 1804. Upon his return to England Coleridge began a series of lectures on poetry and Shakespeare, which are now considered the basis of his reputation as a literary critic. Because of Coleridge's abuse of opium and alcohol, his erratic behavior caused him to quarrel with Wordsworth, and he left Keswick to return to London. In the last years of his life Coleridge wrote political and philosophical works, and his *Biographia Literaria,* considered his greatest critical writing, in which he developed artistic theories that were intended to be the introduction to a great philosophical work. Coleridge died in 1834 of complications stemming from his dependence on opium.

Poem Summary

Lines 1-4

The poem opens with a simple factual statement: An old sailor stops one of three men walking by who are on their way to a wedding. The fact that he chooses only one individual out of the three will be mentioned again at the end of the poem. The dialogue begins at line three with the guest asking the old man why he has stopped him. He also comments on the Mariner's glittering eye, a detail that will be repeated twice more in the first six stanzas. Lines 2 and 4 are exemplary of Coleridge's use of archaic words: "stoppeth" and "stopp'st."

Note

An Ancient Mariner meeteth three Gallants bidden to a wedding-feast and detaineth one.

Lines 5-8

The focus of these lines is on the guest's desires and responsibilities. He is the groom's closest relative, so it is his duty to attend the wedding and the feast that follows.

Lines 9-16

Coleridge uses the following two stanzas to illustrate the power of the Mariner's gaze. Although the Mariner physically restrains the guest in line 9, he drops his hand quickly when challenged. Line 13 explains that his true power thus lies in the hypnotic quality of his gaze and not in his physical strength. The guest is transfixed like prey held fast by the unblinking stare of a predator; his will is surrendered to the Ancient Mariner.

Note

The Wedding-Guest is spell-bound by the eye of the old sea-faring man, and constrained to hear his tale.

Lines 17-24

Like many Gothic tales, the story opens with an ordinary setting—the wedding guest is on his way to a joyous, but ordinary, function—when suddenly he is trapped by the Mariner and his tale. The Mariner's own story begins in a very ordinary, and somewhat similar, manner—the ship sets off, and the entire town celebrates the joyous occasion. Soon, however, the Mariner's tale changes from the realm of everyday activity into the world of spirits and the supernatural. In this retelling, he will bring the guest along on his journey.

Lines 25-30

The sun, which will later be shown to be an

important symbol, is used to convey geographic details accurately. Coleridge's note reinforces this point. Because the sun rises on the left side of the boat, the reader knows the vessel is heading south. Coleridge's details about geography and nature are frequently quite specific and for the most part accurate. Thus, the farther south the ship goes, the more directly overhead the sun will be. For Coleridge, the "line" always refers to the equator.

Note

The maniner tells how the ship sailed southward with a good wind and fair weather, till it reached the line.

Lines 31-36

The focus of the poem returns to the world of the ordinary, to the wedding, with its music and celebration. The wedding guest beats his breast, symbolizing his frustration and longing to attend the wedding as he hears the music playing.

Note

The Wedding-Guest heareth the bridal music; but the Mariner continueth his tale.

Lines 37-40

Repetition is often an important poetic element in ballads. Here, Coleridge uses it to reinforce the power of the Mariner's gaze. The wedding guest is trapped by a power he cannot resist. Line 37 repeats line 31; although he beats his breast, he cannot break the Mariner's spell. Lines 38 to 40 are also a repetition, of lines 18 to 20.

Lines 41-44

Up to this point, the voyage has been normal, but then a storm sets in. Coleridge uses personification, attributing human characteristics to that which is not human, when he describes the storm as a tyrant chasing the ship. The feeling conveyed is such that it seems that a malevolent force has deliberately targeted this ship.

Note

The ship drawn by a storm toward the South Pole.

Lines 45-50

Varying the stanza length and rhyme scheme, Coleridge makes the lines of poetry flee just like the ship.

Lines 51-57

In these stanzas, the ship enters a totally new and frightening world of mystery and cold. The strangeness of the environment is developed with a series of vivid images: emerald icebergs, ice that moans and cries, lifeless vistas. While these may sound fantastic, even to a modern reader, John Livingston Lowes, in his *The Road to Xanadu: A Study in the Ways of the Imagination,* reinforces the accuracy of Coleridge's details by providing several sources on which he based these descriptions. In addition, the development of an atmosphere of uncertainty and imminent danger in an unnatural setting is a common element in Gothic literature.

Note

The land of ice, and of fearful sounds, where no living thing was to be seen.

Lines 58-62

Line 58 indicates that the ship is surrounded by ice. The next line reinforces it. Coleridge repeats the word ice four times in lines 58 to 60, so that the lines themselves are filled with ice.

Lines 63-66

Coleridge stages a dramatic introduction by making the albatross materialize out of the fog. It soon becomes apparent that the albatross plays a key role in the poem, though many critics differ on its importance. He is seen by some as merely a bird, while others view him as a Jesus-like figure. In lines 65 and 66 the albatross is greeted as a Christian soul, hailed in God's name.

Note

Till a great sea-bird, called the Albatross, came through the snow-fog, and was received with great joy and hospitality.

Lines 67-74

These lines further discuss the special relationship between the bird—the only living creature seen in the land of ice—and the crew. They offer the bird hospitality and encourage it to remain with them. Shortly thereafter there is a split in the ice. Coleridge's marginal gloss explains that the bird is a good omen.

Note

And lo! The Albatross proveth a bird of good omen, and followeth the ship as it returned northward through fog and floating ice.

Lines 75-77

Coleridge emphasizes the loyalty of the albatross that comes each evening to sit on the ship. Vespers are evening prayers said by Catholics, but they also may refer to the evening.

Line 78

Coleridge introduces the moonlight in this line. The moon will later assume an important symbolic role in the poem.

Lines 79-82

Without any apparent motive or reason, the Mariner shoots and kills the albatross. Part 1 of the poem ends very abruptly, as it began, with this event. It is possible to interpret the Mariner's act in many ways: a simple violation of hospitality, a symbolic act of murder, a recreation of Adam's fall in the Garden of Eden, or a reenactment of the crucifixion of Christ.

Note

The Ancient Mariner inhospitably killeth the pious bird of good omen.

Lines 83-86

In these lines, Coleridge reverses lines 25 to 28 as to indicate a change in the ship's direction as it heads north. The reader is now as aware as the Mariner of the details of the voyage. The ship has passed Cape Horn, the southernmost part of South America. The word "Sun" is now capitalized, indicating that it is symbolically important.

Lines 87-90

The second stanza in this section reiterates the details of lines 71 through 74. The contrast, however, now has a far more important emotional meaning, for the sense of joy in the earlier lines has been destroyed. The crew is once again alone on the empty seas, and the bird's absence constantly reminds them of their isolation; there are no other living creatures around.

Lines 91-102

These two longer stanzas that describe the crew's changing attitude are very important because they implicate the crew for the Mariner's sin. Although the crew at first denounces the Mariner, describing his deed as hellish, they applaud the killing of the albatross after the sun shines through the polar mists. The marginal note explains that with the crew's betrayal, they participate in the Mariner's sin.

It is ironic that the appearance of the sun causes the change of attitude of the crew. Although Coleridge describes the sun as glorious in line 98, it will soon change.

Note

His shipmates cry out against the Ancient Mariner for killing the bird of good luck.

But when the fog cleared off, they justify the same, and thus make themselves accomplices in the crime.

Lines 103-106

In these lines, Coleridge describes the ship's passage into the Pacific Ocean using sound to reinforce his meaning. The alliteration in this stanza begins a light "f" sound: "fair," "free," "flew." It is then accompanied by the more forceful "b" sound: "burst," "blew." The words themselves convey the airy, floating sense of the breeze. Lines 103 to 105 describe the ship as returning to normal conditions, but the description of the silent sea in line 106 hints at the impending disaster. Though it is unclear in the poem, the marginal note informs the reader that the ship continues north until it reaches the equator.

Note

The fiar breeze continues; the ship enters the Pacific Ocean and sails northward, even till it reaches the line.

Lines 107-110

The wind stops and leaves the crew motionless, indicating that their punishment is close at hand. Coleridge also alliterates the "s" sound.

Note

The ship hath been suddenly becalmed.

Lines 111-114

Coleridge provides many powerful images to convey the ship's plight. He describes the sky, for example, as hot and copper. Copper is an excellent conductor of heat, and thus magnifies the waves of heat that are beating down upon the crew. The sun has now turned bloody instead of glorious.

Lines 115-118

Coleridge repeats the phrase "day after day" to emphasize the passage of time. A simile in lines 117 and 118 reinforces the stillness; the ship has no more movement than a ship in a picture.

Lines 119-122

This powerful image emphasizes the lack of fresh water. The boards are shrinking because the heat and absence of fresh water to moisten them. It is ironic that the crew virtually dies of thirst while they are surrounded by an endless expanse of undrinkable saltwater.

Note

And the Albatross begins to be avenged.

Lines 123-126

Coleridge evokes a nightmarish description of rot and decay. Water is typically a life–giving force, but in line 123 it decays. Later, in lines 129 and 130, it burns. The repetition of "slimy" adds to the unpleasant imagery. Coleridge chooses the word "things" to describe the crawling creatures. The very vagueness of the term indicates that these are so unpleasant that they have no name. Lowes, seeking the source for such creatures, found travel books that mention seas rotting with sea weed, slime fish, and burning water. This description, however, is used for its nightmarish quality rather than its accuracy.

Lines 127-130

Coleridge emphasizes the supernatural quality of the burning water by using the simile "like witch's oils."

Lines 131-134

The punishment is given by a spirit from the land of the albatross. The marginal note discusses at length the nature of these invisible spirits.

Note

A Spirit had followed them; one of the invisible inhabitants of this planet, neither departed souls nor angels; concerning whom the learned Jew, Josephus, and the Platonic Constantinopolitan, Michael Psellus, may be consulted. They are very numerous, and there is no climate or element without one or more.

Lines 135-138

Coleridge vividly describes the suffering of the

entire crew.

Lines 139-142

The cross is apparently a symbol of Christ. The cross around the Mariner's neck is replaced by the albatross, a highly symbolic action. Again, there are many different interpretations of this act. First, the Mariner may no longer deserve to wear the cross of Christianity and must replace it with the symbol of his sin. Second, he figuratively carries the albatross around his neck as Christ carried the cross. The marginal note explains that the crew wishes to throw the guilt totally on the mariner. Thus, like Christ, he bears the guilt for all.

Note

The shipmates, in their sore distress, would fain throw the whole guilt on the Ancient Mariner: in sign whereof they hang the dead sea-bird round his neck.

Lines 143-148

Part 3 is the most Gothic section of the entire poem, full of nightmarish images and supernatural beings. The stanzas themselves are the most varied here, as the unsettling images distort everything, including the structure of the poem itself. The six lines in the first stanza emphasize the words weary and glazed. Everything is dull and devoid of hope unlike the glittering gaze of the Mariner in the opening stanzas. Coleridge's marginal notes in this section are particularly helpful in comprehending the poem.

Note

The Ancient Mariner beholdeth a sign in the element afar off.

Lines 149-156

Repetition is used to signal the Mariner's growing hope as the dot in the distance draws closer.

Lines 157-161

Because there is no water, the crew cannot speak. The Mariner sacrifices himself by biting his arm and drinking his own blood and notifying the crew of the approaching ship.

Note

At its nearer approach it seemeth him to be a ship; and at a dear ransom he freeth his speech from the bonds of thirst.

Lines 162-170

Coleridge contrasts the initial joy of the crew at the thought of rescue with the fear that follows when they realize that the ship is moving by some supernatural power.

Note

A flash of joy;

And horror follows. For can it be a ship that comes onward without wind or tide?

Lines 171-176

Coleridge's vivid description of nature reinforces the mood as the sun lights up the western sky with flames. This red backdrop highlights the ghostly ship that approaches. In the next four stanzas and accompanying note, Coleridge will repeat "Sun" six times as he describes the ship that has appeared between the Mariner and the sun.

Lines 177-184

The note stresses the skeletal nature of the ship. Although the Mariner begs Mary for grace here, he will soon discover himself unable to pray.

Note

It seemeth him but the skeleton of a ship.

Lines 185-194

Coleridge continues to develop Gothic visions as he further describes the skeleton ship. As the vessel approaches, the Mariner wonders about its inhabitants. In the marginal note, Coleridge answers the Mariner's questions.

Coleridge's description of the woman is puzzling. Red lips, golden hair, and fair skin are considered signs of beauty, and the phrase "Her looks were free" implies sexual awareness. The woman on the vessel, however, is hideous. Contrast the use of color in this description with that of the bride in line 24. While the bride's redness is compared to that of a rose, the white of Spectre-Woman's skin bears the decay of leprosy.

Note

And its ribs are seen as bars on the face of the setting Sun. The Spectre-Woman and her Deathmate and no other on board the skeleton ship.

Like vessel, like crew!

Lines 195-198

It is necessary to read the note here in order to understand the nature of the stakes in this dice game between death and death-in-life. The victory of death-in-life explains the Mariner's unique fate. He is condemned to suffer endlessly, without ever having death to end the suffering.

Note

Death and life-Death have diced for the ship's

crew, and she (the latter) winneth the Ancient Mariner.

Lines 199-202

Night falls suddenly, as Coleridge's note explains, since there is no period of twilight at the equator.

Note

No twilight within the courts of the Sun.

Lines 203-211

Coleridge's vivid images render this night as particularly mysterious and dark. His use of the metaphor "thick" to describe the night magnifies the fearfulness and darkness of the waiting. When the crescent moon rises, it appears with one star: the planet Venus.

Lines 212-223

Coleridge stresses the death of each crewman, "one after one," in order to intensify the devastating effect this has on the Mariner. Although each dies without a word, they turn to curse the Mariner with a look. When the spirits leave the dead bodies "one by one," each spirit reminds the Mariner of his sin as they pass "like the whizz of my crossbow."

Note

At the rising of the Moon,
One after another,
His shipmates drop down dead;
But Life-in Death begins her work
on the Ancient
Mariner.

Lines 224-231

Coleridge begins Part 4 with the Mariner pausing his tale of horror and returning the focus on the confounded guest. This has the effect of lessening the tension after the extremely dramatic, supernatural life and death quality of Part 3.

Note

The Wedding-Guest feareth that a spirit is talking to him;

But the Ancient Mariner assureth him of his of his bodily life, and proceedeth to relate his horrible penance.

Lines 232-235

Repetition of the word "alone" reinforces the Mariner's sense of isolation.

Lines 236-243

In this stanza, Coleridge contrasts the beauty of the men while they were alive with the multitude of slimy creatures in the sea. Because he lives, the Mariner feels that he is a part of the world of slime and decay that surrounds him. Several critics stress the importance of Coleridge's note that the Mariner's despising the sea creatures and himself indicates that he despises nature itself, and thus has learned nothing.

Note

He despiseth the creatures of the calm.

And envieth that they should live, and so many lie dead.

Lines 244-247

With this stanza, Coleridge emphasizes a key Christian symbol: souls that are damned are unable to pray. The Mariner's soul, too, is rotting like everything else around him.

Lines 248-262

Coleridge describes the Mariner's torment, again using the image of the weary eye. He cannot avoid the eyes of the dead men, and accepts their curse as he feels that he is the one who brought about this destruction.

Media Adaptations

- *English Romantic Poetry,* read by Sir Ralph Richardson, Claire Bloom, Sir Anthony Quayle, and Frederick Worlock includes "The Rime of the Ancient Mariner" and "Kubla Khan" by Coleridge, Harper Caedmon.

  Many of Coleridge's poems are accessible on the World Wide Web. The S.T. Coleridge Home Page URL is http://www.lib.virginia.edu/etext/stc/Col A very comprehensive listing of other Samuel Taylor Coleridge resources on the Internet is available at http://www.lib.virginia.edu/etext/stc/Col

Note

But the curse liveth for him in the eye of the dead men.

Lines 263-271

Coleridge fills this section with contrasting images: the moon travels gently in its path, welcomed everywhere, while the ship is trapped in the burning water; the moon is described as cool and restful, while the ship is described as red and filled with heat. Again the color red is used, but this time it connotes hell-fire and terror.

Note

In his loneliness and fixedness he yearneth towards the journeying moon, and the Stars that still sojourn yet still more onward; and everywhere the blue sky belongs to them, and is their appointeed rest, and their native country and their own natural homes, which they enter unannounced, as lords that are certainly expected and yet there is a silent joy at their arrival.

Lines 272-276

Coleridge continues contrasting images with vivid descriptions in the next two stanzas. Beyond the shadow of the ship, the water snakes seem to shimmer in the moonlight that reflects off of them as they move.

Note

Lines 277-281

In the ship's shadow, however, the water snakes take on an even more beautiful aspect as they glow with color and light. This is a large contrast from the ship's presentation as a place of desolation and despair after the death of the albatross. The color red had previously conveyed images of fire and death, but in line 281, the tracks of the snakes flash with "golden fire," a phrase that is warm and comforting. This shift foreshadows the change which will occur in the Mariner himself in the next stanza.

Lines 282-287

Part 4 ends with the freeing of the Mariner's soul. He blesses the snakes, "unaware" of the forgiveness bestowed on him.

Note

Lines 288-291

Once he is forgiven, the Mariner can pray

again. As he prays, the enormous weight of the albatross and his crime is released. Coleridge uses the simile "like lead" to convey the enormous burden which is now lifted.

Note

The spell begins to break.

Lines 292-296

As Part 5 begins, Coleridge uses a series of images to convey the peace and comfort that comes to the Mariner; he is finally able to sleep.

Lines 297-308

When the Mariner dreams of rain, it rains. He feels light in his body and soul. This atmosphere is in contrast to the previous section where there was a predominance of weariness, loneliness, and decay.

Note

By grace of the holy Mother, the Ancient Mariner is refreshed with rain.

Lines 309-317

The calm and quiet of the last verses disappear as the Mariner is surrounded by strange sights and sounds. The fires in the sky, which make the stars seem pale in comparison, sound like the Aurora

Borealis. It would make geographical sense if this were the case, since the ship must leave the Pacific and round Cape Horn at the tip of South America again in order for the Mariner to return home. Coleridge does not stress the geography, but his awareness of it in other parts of the poem makes this a possibility. The fires may also be seen as a manifestation of the spirit world.

Note

He heareth sounds and seeth strange sights and commotions in the sky and the element.

Lines 318-326

Coleridge uses vivid imagery to describe the supernatural phenomena in this storm.

Note

The bodies of the ship's crew are inspired, and the ship moves on;

Lines 327-340

These lines demonstrate more examples of Gothic influences on the story. When the dead return to life and the Mariner assumes his place beside them, there is a deep sense of terror and oppression.

Lines 341-344

Coleridge adds a very poignant quality to the tale with these lines. Perhaps more than any other in the poem, they serve to remind the reader of the normal world to which the Mariner once belonged. It is ironic that he is seen as having a family only after he is forced to work next to his nephew, with whom there is no longer any possibility of love or communication.

Lines 345-349

The ghastly quality of the story frightens the guest. When the Mariner reassures him that the spirits who possessed the dead are "blest," it contrasts the picture of them in line 340 as "a ghastly crew."

Note

but not by the souls of the men, nor by daemons of earth or middle air, but by a blessed troop of angelic spirits sent down by the invocation of the guardian saint.

Lines 350-357

The contrast continues in these lines. When the dead first rose, they groaned (a typical Gothic detail). As the day dawns, the spirits become music, creating a marvelous mixture of sounds and notes. In these lines, sound and music are used to create a sense of peace. Another interesting contrast is with the spirits that gather around the mast at dawn: before its death the albatross perched there every evening.

Lines 358-366

Coleridge uses natural and musical imagery to convey the beauty of the music the Mariner hears.

Lines 367-372

After the music of the spirits ceases, Coleridge continues using sound imagery, creating a simile: the sails sound like a hidden brook providing a lullaby to the wood. Interestingly, Coleridge uses sound to convey a sense of quiet.

Lines 373-382

Coleridge supplies details about the voyage itself in these two stanzas and in the accompanying note that explain how the ship moves without a breeze. The Spirit of snow and ice is carrying the ship from below. The note makes it clear that this spirit resents helping the Mariner and wants him to receive further punishment for the murder of the albatross.

Note

The lonesome Spirit from the South Pole carries on the ship as far as the Line, in obedience to the angelic troop, but still requireth vengeance.

Lines 383-392

Coleridge once again reestablishes clear geographic details with a metaphor. The sun, straight above the mast, pins the ship to the water at the equator. When the ship moves again, the motion causes the Mariner to faint.

Lines 393-405

When the Mariner regains partial consciousness, he hears the voices of spirits. Coleridge uses these voices to review the details of the poem. The note identifies the speakers as fellow daemons of the Polar Spirit. The word daemon is not the same as the modern word, demon. Rather, daemons are invisible spirits, living in the world. They may be patterned after similar spirits in Greek mythology who lived in nature, serving as messengers between the gods and man. The first voice restates the Mariner's sin. The gentle albatross loved and trusted the Mariner, who shot him. The reference to Jesus in line 399 serves to reinforce the Christian symbolism of the albatross.

Note

The Polar Spirit's fellow daemons, the invisible inhabitants of the element, take part in his wrong; and two of them relate, one to the other, that penance long and heavy for the Ancient Mariner hath been accorded to the Polar Spirit, who returneth southward.

Lines 406-409

This final stanza in Part 5 foreshadows the rest of the poem. The peace of this section is only transitory; the Mariner will suffer more.

Lines 410-413 ✳ PART 6

Coleridge continues to use the spirit voices to clarify the poem for the reader. In lines 411 through 439, they explain how the ship is moving.

Lines 414-417

The second voice points out the still ocean that is waiting for directions from the Moon. Line 414 contains a simile in which there is a slave before a master, that is used to illustrate the calm.

Lines 418-421

Since the moon controls the tides, it gives the ocean its direction.

Note

The Mariner hath been cast into a trance; for the angelic power causeth the vessel to drive northward faster than human life could endure.

Lines 422-429

In answer to the repeated query, the second voice explains that the ship is being driven by a power that parts the air so that it may pass through. The marginal note adds that this is an angelic power, and that the ship is moving so swiftly that the Mariner could not survive if he were fully conscious.

Lines 430-441

PART 6

Coleridge returns to the Gothic imagery of Part 3, providing a distinct contrast to the peaceful descriptions of Part 5. As the Mariner wakes, he finds the dead men staring at him. He describes them as fit for a "charnel-dungeon"—a place where dead bodies are kept. The moonlight, usually peaceful, is reflected in their eyes. As the guest is trapped by the Mariner's stare, so too is the Mariner transfixed by the dead men. These lines also recall Part 4 when the Mariner finds himself momentarily unable to pray.

Note

The supernatural motion is retarded; the Mariner awakes, and his penance begins anew.

Lines 432-445

The spell is broken and the Mariner can look to the ocean.

Note

The curse is finally expiated.

Lines 446-451

Coleridge uses a powerful extended simile that continues throughout the six-line stanza to describe the Mariner's fear about what may lie ahead of him.

Lines 452-459

The wind returns, but now it is a supernatural force that touches only the Mariner and not the objects around him.

Lines 460-463

There is an alliteration of "swiftly" and "sweetly" in lines 460 and 462. In fact, the entire stanza contains many instances of alliteration.

Lines 464-467

The Mariner sees his home. For consistency, Coleridge is careful to mention the landmarks in the reverse order from which he first described them during the ship's farewell in lines 23 and 24.

Note

And the Ancient Mariner beholdeth his native country.

Lines 468-471

In these lines, the Mariner's questions emphasize his disbelief that he is truly home. He prays that if this is only a dream, it will be one from which he will never waken.

Lines 472-479

The moon provides a benevolent guiding light revealing to the Mariner his home in a series of vivid images.

Lines 480-487

The crimson shapes filling the bay in the moonlight seem to be living, supernatural creatures. They may be the daemons or spirits of the Mariner's own land. Nevertheless, these beings have played a prominent role in the Mariner's voyage all along.

Note

The angelic spirits leave the dead bodies, and appear in their own forms of light.

Lines 488-499

The spirits within the crew leave and the Mariner sees that they are angels. They bid the Mariner farewell and, in their silence, bless the Mariner. The phrase "By the holy rood" refers to the crucifix.

Lines 500-507

With the sound of oars, Coleridge reintroduces the ordinary world. The Mariner recognizes the voices of people he knew, and the supernatural realm vanishes. His happiness is so great that even the realization that he, alone, is returning from the voyage cannot diminish it.

Lines 508-513

Coleridge includes the hermit as the third passenger in the boat. Part 6 ends with the Mariner's hope that this good man will forgive his sins.

Lines 514-522

Coleridge opens Part 7 with a description of the hermit: a good man who lives in harmony with God, man, and nature. These characteristics are important since the Mariner has been out of harmony with all three.

Note

The Hermit of the wood approacheth the ship with wonder.

Lines 523-526

The lights from the seraph band had drawn the men toward the ship. Now that the angels have departed, the ship lies in darkness.

Lines 527-537

As the three men approach the ship, they are shocked by its ragged condition. Coleridge uses a simile comparing the ship's sails to leaves in the winter.

Lines 538-541

In these lines, Coleridge contrasts the fear of the pilot with the open-hearted optimism of the hermit.

Lines 542-549

For the last time, the world of the supernatural intrudes. There is a sound under the water and the the bay splits open. The ship then disappears exactly as the albatross disappeared: "like lead." Gothic literature is filled with similar visions where the earth splits so that people and objects can be dragged down beneath the earth.

Note

The ship suddenly sinketh.

Lines 550-559

The Mariner, thrown clear, is rescued by the boat as the hills reverberate with sound. The little boat is caught up in the whirlpool created by the sunken ship.

Note

The Ancient Mariner is saved in the Pilot's boat.

Lines 560-569

The three rescuers thought the Mariner was dead, and are horrified when he begins to speak and move.

Lines 570-577

On land, the Mariner begs the hermit to forgive him.

Note

The Ancient Mariner earnestly entreateth the Hermit to shrive him; and the penance of life falls on him.

Lines 578-581

The Mariner is handed his punishment: he is forced by an uncontrollable urge to tell his story.

Lines 582-590

The Mariner is forced to travel from land to

land searching for certain individuals to whom he must relate his story. This is why he stopped the guest. It was his destiny was to hear the tale and to learn from the Mariner's suffering.

Critics have found parallels between the ancient Mariner and Cain, who was forced to wander the earth after the murder of his brother, Abel. He has also been compared to the legendary figure of the Wandering Jew, who was supposedly so cruel to Christ during the crucifixion that he is forced to wander the earth forever.

Note

And ever and anon throughout his future life an agony constraineth him to travel from land to land,

Lines 591-596

The poem returns to the present, where the wedding ceremony is over. It is the Mariner who mentions this, now that his tale has been told. The guest offers no protests and seems unaware of the wedding feast.

Lines 597-600

The Mariner repeats line 234 to remind the guest of the terrible isolation that he went through, where he was separated from all other living things. Even God seemed absent from him.

Lines 601-609

The Mariner reminds the guest of the simple pleasure that comes in prayerful company.

Lines 610-617

In these lines, Coleridge states the moral of the poem: that one must necessarily love all living things. Many critics object to this simple message, Coleridge, himself, being among them.

Note

and to teach, by his own example, love and reverence to all things that God made and loveth.

Lines 618-625

The Mariner, his eye still bright, disappears, leaving the last stanzas of the poem to the wedding guest. No longer interested in the wedding feast, he holds still within the trance of the Mariner's gaze. The poem ends with the guest having learned the Mariner's lesson.

Themes

Sin

The poem "The Rime of the Ancient Mariner" revolves around a single action, the killing of a bird, known as the albatross, and its horrible consequences. The repercussions of the Mariner's crime are puzzling at first. However cruel the killing might have been, why should two hundred men die and the Mariner himself be driven nearly insane as a result?

But the Mariner's action cannot be judged in these simple terms, for it is far more than a secular crime, like robbing a bank or even killing a man. That the murder is deeply religious in nature is shown when the dead albatross is equated with Christ: "Instead of the cross, the Albatross / About my neck was hung," the Mariner says. Killing the bird was more than an ordinary crime because it violated the sacred natural order, an order encompassing the visible and the invisible, the spiritual, the natural, and the human. It included the Polar Spirit and other spirits, the albatross, the ice and sea and sun and moon, as well as the men on the ship. All are bound by an intricate series of connections, of which the Ancient Mariner is completely unaware. He is able to kill the albatross without a thought. But like Adam's sin, the simple act of eating an apple, the Mariner's violence calls

Environmental issue. — tody.

for a harsh punishment.

Like the biblical Adam, who ate the apple because he wanted to be like God himself, the Mariner places himself on a par with God above nature. As far as he is concerned, humans are the measure of all things. In such an order, he can kill the bird without a second thought; to him, there is no deeper moral order. It is clear after the other sailors have died that the Mariner feels mankind is better than the rest of nature. Looking at the sea, he regrets the deaths of "the many men so beautiful" while "a thousand thousand slimy things," the ocean creatures, still live. The Ancient Mariner will not begin atoning for his sin until realizes that he is not master of the world, but part of it. — *Hermit is in harmony with world.*

Atonement

Like the story of Adam and Eve, the Mariner's sin is eventually followed by redemption. Gazing at the ocean, he sees schools of sea snakes glistening in the moonlight. They are no longer "slimy things," they are bathed in beautiful "golden fire." "A spring of love gushed from my heart, / And I blessed them unaware." This moment is the poem's turning point and it mirrors the casual, ignorant murder of the bird.

It might seem odd that such a moment could save him. What is important is that his essential nature has changed, the nature that led him to kill the albatross in the first place. The Mariner realizes that he had nothing to do with that change—it was a

gift from a higher power. "Sure my kind saint took pity on me / And I blessed them unaware," he says. \
No one can *choose* to love. Love is a gift that springs from the heart; we either love or we do not.

The instant he blesses the water snakes, he is saved and can return home. His punishment has been severe: the death of his crew, thirst, and fearful visions. But he continues to carry his guilt with him, even after his redemption. When the Mariner returns to his country, he turns to the hermit. "He'll shrieve my soul, he'll wash away / The Albatross's blood." He confesses his guilt to the hermit. But after he has been forgiven, the Mariner's atonement continues. By the end of the poem, he "hath penance done and penance more will do." So the Mariner wanders the earth telling his story, to "teach" others.

Imagination

Imagination plays a special role in "The Rime of the Ancient Mariner." In the poem imagination has transformative powers. It is a special form of knowledge more true and insightful than other forms. The sailors employ a scientific approach to life and therefore misconstrue many of the spiritual events and their consequences. misunderstood

When the Mariner kills the albatross, for example, and the ship begins to drift through the fog, he says, "all averred, I had killed the bird / That made the breeze to blow." But the next day the "glorious sun" rises and the sailors change their tune. "Then all averred, I had killed the bird that brought the fog and mist." Their reasoning is superficial and fails to go beyond their own limited momentary self-interest. It lacks any broader moral basis.

The Mariner and his men have unwittingly sailed into a universe full of spirits and ghostly ships and roaring ice that cannot be known by the common modes of perception. No one on the ship is aware of the deeper realities that surround the ship. The Mariner does not realize the albatross's place in the mysterious unseen order and he kills it. He does not understand his *own* place in the world. The world he finds himself in cannot be grasped by mere reason. It has the shape and feel of a dream where the rules of logic no longer apply. It can only be grasped by the imagination.

In the poem imagination is represented by wind blowing and moonlight shining down on the sea. The first sign is the appearance of the albatross, "the bird that made the breeze to blow." The Mariner kills the bird, and his punishment is to be eventually left alone on a rotting ship, the rest of the crew dead.

The world without imagination is a dead world, and it is a world the Mariner chooses because of his murder of the bird. The spirit of imagination is there, in the form of the Polar Spirit deep below the water. The Polar Spirit is like the creative spirit; it comes unseen and may be benign or destructive. The Mariner is like a dead man himself, doomed to "death-in-life." The Mariner finally turns in disgust from the empty world around him. "I closed my eyes, and kept them closed … for the sky and the sea and the sea and the sky / Lay like a load on my weary eye / And the dead men at my feet."

The doors to imagination open for the Mariner when he turns his back on the superficial world of sensory perception. The moon rises, new light shines, and a different world is revealed. The creatures of the sea look so different that normal, logical speech does not describe them. They can only be experienced directly. "Oh happy living things! No tongue / Their beauty might declare."

After his experience in the moonlight, the Mariner realizes that there is a moral order in the universe. He knows that that order encompasses him and every other creature.

When the spirit of the air says "the Spirit who bideth by himself *In the land of mist and snow,* He loved the bird that loved the man / Who shot him with his bow," it is describing an unending chain of love that binds all beings. The Mariner's senseless murder broke that chain. Afterward, wandering the earth, he remains intensely sensitive to this awareness and tries to communicate it to the Wedding Guest. The most important thing, he asserts, is to worship God.

Topics for Further Study

- The Mariner of this poem is sent out to travel the world and teach about love and reverence. Imagine this happening now. What occupation, other than mariner, might be given a person responsible for this chore? Since albatrosses are rare today, what other crime against nature might a contemporary person commit to bring this punishment upon him or herself? Write a scenario that would retain the emotions of guilt and redemption from this poem, but transfer them to the world in which you live.

- The third section of the poem concerns the approach of the skeleton ship, with Death and Death-in-Life coming to meet the Ancient Mariner. To what extent is he glad to see them? Has his loneliness increased his interest in the macabre? How can you tell? What do the details of their appearance tell the Mariner he can expect out of life in the future?

Alienation and Loneliness

The Ancient Mariner is an outsider. He leaves his countrymen to sail off into the unknown. He is confronted with real isolation for the first time when ice traps the ship in the south polar seas. "Nor shapes of men nor beasts we ken / The ice was all between." The spell of isolation is broken by the arrival of the bird. The seamen greet it "as if it had been a Christian soul" and share their food with it. It remains with them and breaks up the ice, eventually enabling the ship to sail free. Once free, the Mariner murders the bird. He is the ultimate outsider, an anti-social outlaw who has violated the most basic rules about hospitality toward guests.

The Mariner's isolation deepens. His shipmates hang the dead bird around his neck as a mark of his exclusion. All communication on the ship ceases and the Mariner is alone in his own thoughts. "Through utter drought all parched we stood." After he hails the ship that bears Death and Death-in-Life, his alienation is total, "alone, alone, all all alone / Alone on the wide wide sea."

The Mariner remains alone on the sea, in a condition one critic has described as schizophrenic. He is on the edge of madness, in such a deep existential crisis that he is alienated from himself as well.

After his mystical experience with the water snakes, he begins to recover from his psychotic trance. Suddenly he is no longer alone, life is everywhere around him and the revelation saves him. "The upper air burst into life!" Suddenly the air is full of music "like all instruments / Now like a lonely flute; / And now it is an angel's song." Even the dead men move again as if they were alive.

The Ancient Mariner is a changed man after his experience but remains alone. He tells the Wedding Guest he values nothing more than the company of other people, yet he wanders the earth alone. He does not join the wedding feast. The effect of the story is to make the Wedding Guest a more lonely, solitary person. He does not join the wedding celebration although he was he was anxious to do so. He simply leaves, "stunned." And it is surely significant that his new-found knowledge not only makes him "a wiser man," but "a sadder" one as well.

"The Rime of the Ancient Mariner" is mostly written in the traditional ballad stanza: a series of fourline verses, the first and third of which are written in iambic tetrameter, and the second and fourth written in iambic trimeter.

In order to analyze the rhythm or meter of a line of poetry, the line must first be divided into syllables. An iamb is a metrical unit consisting of one unstressed syllable followed by one stressed syllable. In Coleridge's poem, for example:

> In **mist** / or **cloud** / on **mast** / or **shroud**
> It **perched** / for **ves** / pers **nine**

When the iambs above are read aloud, the emphasis falls on every second syllable. The meter of the first line is in iambic tetrameter because it contains four iambic units in each line (totalling eight syllables), whereas the meter of the second line is in iambic trimeter because it contains only three iambic units (totalling six syllables).

Ballad stanzas also employ a set rhyme scheme. In the traditional schematic form, the second and the fourth lines rhyme, whereas the first and third lines do not. Coleridge followed this pattern, frequently adding additional rhyming elements. In the lines above, "cloud" and "shroud" are examples of internal rhyme, because they rhyme within a single line. Furthermore, the line contains alliteration, a rhyming element that repeats the beginning sounds of words (e.g. "mist" and "mast"). Coleridge also uses the rhyming element assonance, in which there are repeated verb sounds within words (e.g. in the second line: "per," "ves," "pers").

Although most of the verses follow the fourline stanza, Coleridge deliberately varies the poem's pattern to illustrate certain points or to help develop an idea, because it calls the reader's attention to a particular section. For example, the first eleven stanzas of the poem follow the basic pattern very closely. In the twelfth stanza, however, both the number of lines and the rhyme scheme change. Of the six lines that form this stanza, the first two employ eye rhyme—"prow" and "blow"— where the words' endings are spelled similarly but differ in their pronunciation. Moreover, Coleridge uses internal rhyme—"fast" and "blast—in the fifth line of this stanza. In this passage, Coleridge also describes the ship as fleeing before the storm. These variations serve to move the poem along more quickly, *i.e.* the lines of poetry themselves speed up or "flee." Coleridge also utilizes stanzaic changes throughout the poem to emphasize his meaning.

The poem is divided into seven parts that are written in dialogue form, with occasional descriptive comments added by the poet. Another important detail in the poem's organization is the inclusion of a series of marginal notes which were added in the 1817 version of the poem. These notes provide a great deal of information—some of which appearing exclusively in the notes—that may help a reader to better understand the poem's sense or meaning.

The French Revolution

In 1798, England was still reacting to the ideas and events of the French Revolution. The French ideology and army both continued to threaten England at that time. The slogan *Liberte, Egalite, Fraternite*—Liberty, Equality, Brotherhood—that inspired the French masses to overthrow, and eventually kill, the French king and queen led the ruling houses of Europe to oppose the French Republic. Bitter opposition to royalty and church, an integral part of France's liberal political philosophy, concerned the conservative rulers of Britain. These radical ideas, it was feared, could lead to unrest in the British lower classes.

France was also a real military threat to Britain. The fear of a French invasion was constant through much of the 1790s. Revolutionary France had threatened to invade neighboring Holland earlier in the decade. In 1796, a French force set out to assist Irish rebels planning an uprising against the English government and only a bad storm kept French troops from landing in Ireland. In 1798, Napoleon massed troops just across the English Channel in preparation for an invasion that never took place.

French intentions seemed clear. England's suspicions spurred many to support the old traditional English values and oppose the new France.

The Irish Rebellion

Britain faced the prospect of revolution in its nearest colony in the second half of the 1790s. Irish Roman Catholics had been demanding religious freedom and reform of the Irish parliament for a few years; and when they went ignored, Irish radicals and members of the working class joined forces to form United Irishmen in 1795. The group was secret, organized along on military lines, and dedicated to radical action in order to reform Ireland. It was also militantly Catholic and targeted its attacks exclusively against Protestants.

Between 1796 and 1798 the situation grew very serious. In 1796, the French attempted an unsuccessful expedition to Ireland with the Irish radical leader Wolfe Tone. As a result of the growing trouble, the English government instituted a series of draconian measures. In 1796 the Insurrection Act was passed, followed by the suspension of the right of *habeas corpus.* The following year the English attempted to seize all private arms in Ireland and suppressed publication of a radical newspaper in Belfast.

In 1798, as the United Irishmen prepared an armed rebellion, the English authorities arrested the main rebel leaders. Local uprisings erupted and a number of battles were fought. In the end, the Irish were defeated at the Battle of Vinegar Hill.

Following their victory, the English government abolished the Irish parliament completely. They allowed the Irish to be represented only in the English parliament.

Compare & Contrast

- **1798:** Napoleon Bonaparte conquers Egypt on July 22, but on August 1 the British navy under Admiral Horatio Nelson destroys the French fleet and strands Bonaparte and his army in Africa.

  Today: The United States together with the United Nations threaten Saddam Hussein and Iraq with sanctions and military action if weapons inspectors are not allowed to inspect key weapon sites.

- **1798:** Irish resistance to British rule is brutally broken at the Battle of Vinegar Hill.

  Today: Ireland and Great Britain continue to try to work out a plan to bring peace to embattled Northern Ireland.

- **1798:** Eli Whitney, the inventor of the cotton gin, develops a system for producing firearms from interchangeable parts. The invention sets the stage for the industrial revolution in America.

  Today: Personal computers, based on the mass-production of silicon chips, are a multibillion dollar industry.

Lyrical Ballads

The publication of *Lyrical Ballads,* a book written by Samuel Taylor Coleridge and William Wordsworth, is considered the beginning of the Romantic movement in English literature. The idea to collaborate on a book of poetry was conceived by Wordsworth and Coleridge at the same time they formulated the idea for the *Ancient Mariner,* a work which was initially planned as a collaboration.

The project was forgotten for three or four months, only to be raised again by Coleridge in 1798. He proposed that they, along with Wordsworth's sister, travel together to Germany in order to learn German, study natural science, and explore German philosophy. The book was intended first and foremost as a way to raise money for the long trip. When *Lyrical Ballads* was published, it opened with "The Rime of the Ancient Mariner"; all but four of its poems were written by Wordsworth.

Lyrical Ballads was revolutionary because it used the language of the working classes. In his preface to the second edition, Wordsworth argued explicitly that this was necessary. He maintained that the language of the lower classes was superior to the elevated, self-consciously poetic language of English poetry. In plain, straightforward language, Wordsworth wrote, "the passions of the heart find a better soil in which they can attain their maturity … and speak in plainer and more emphatic language."

That essay became a manifesto for other Romantic poets. In the aftermath of the French Revolution, the essay and the poetry in *Lyrical Ballads* was viewed as incendiary and dangerous by some critics. It was dangerous because by leveling the language of different social classes, the book implied a similar leveling of *all* class distinctions. It was perceived to oppose to the age-old English system of noble and subject. Wordsworth wrote that through the ability to feel the "great and simple affections" of human nature—an ability this common language conferred—"one being is elevated above another."

Critical Overview

Nineteenth-century critics had somewhat mixed reviews regarding "The Rime of the Ancient Mariner." They lauded the poem's brilliant imagery, but found the story unconvincing, the language distracting, and the theme incomprehensible. Twentieth-century critics cannot agree on a standard interpretation of the poem. In *The Road to Xanadu,* John Livingston Lowes argues that the moral of the poem only has validity within the special world that Coleridge created. He notes, however, that the death of an entire crew is a rather harsh punishment for the death of a bird. Lowes contends that the poem operates on three "interlocking" levels: the voyage, the spirit world, and the tale of crime and punishment. He fails, however, to regard the poem's effectiveness as a tale of salvation and redemption. Nevertheless, Lowes's greatest contribution to the study of "The Ancient Mariner" is his intensive investigation into Coleridge's sources that sparked a renewed interest in his poetry.

In "A Poem of Pure Imagination," Robert Penn Warren disagrees with Lowes's views on the triviality of the Mariner's act, contending that the poem's primary theme is one of sacramental vision; of "One Life" for all creatures. The Mariner's crime represents humankind's fall from grace, like original sin. Warren also points out that "the bird is hailed 'in God's name,' both literally and symbolically, and in the end we have, therefore, in the crime against Nature a crime against God." For Coleridge, then, God is nature, and in doing this act, the Mariner separates himself from nature and ultimately from God. In *Coleridge: The Clark Lectures,* Humphry House discusses the importance of Coleridge's use of natural imagery in developing the poem's main theme. He points out that the elements of nature not only provide key insights into the Mariner's spiritual state, but they also provide "the link between the Mariner as an ordinary man, and the Mariner as one acquainted with the invisible world, which has its own sets of values." House cautions the reader against wholeheartedly adopting any single interpretation of the poem, as he contends that any such action may limit, and ultimately prevent, the reader from gaining valuable insight from issues that he may have overlooked.

Sources

Boulger, James D., *Twentieth Century Interpretations of The Rime of the Ancient Mariner,* Prentice Hall, Inc., 1969.

Empson, William, "The Ancient Mariner: An Answer to Warren," in *Kenyon Review,* Winter, 1993, pp. 155-77.

House, Humphry, in *Coleridge: The Clark Lectures, 1951-52,* Rupert Hart-Davis, 1953, 167 p.

Knox-Shaw, P. H., "The Eastern Ancient Mariner," in *Essays in Criticism,* April, 1996, pp. 115-35.

Lowes, John Livingston, in *The Road to Xanadu: A Study in the Ways of the Imagination,* Houghton-Mifflin Company, 1927, 639 p.

Stevenson, Warren, "The Case of the Missing Captain," in *The Wordsworth Circle,* Winter, 1995, pp. 12-18.

Warren, Robert Penn, "A Poem of Pure Imagination: An Experiment in Reading," in *The Rime of the Ancient Mariner* by Samuel Taylor Coleridge, Reynal and Hitchcock, 1946, pp. 59-117.

Watkins, Daniel P., "History as Demon in Coleridge's *The Rime of the Ancient Mariner,*" in *Papers on Language and Literature,* Vol. 24, No. 1, Winter 1988.

Williams, Anne, "An I for an Eye," in *PMLA,* October, 1993, pp. 1114-127.

Wordsworth, William, and Samuel Taylor Coleridge, *Lyrical Ballads,* Methuen, 1968.

For Further Study

Buchan, A. M., "The Sad Wisdom of the Mariner," in *Twentieth Century Interpretations of The Rime of the Ancient Mariner,* Englewood Cliffs, NJ: Prentice Hall, Inc., 1969.

> An accessible essay that considers deeper implications of the killing of the Albatross, and the guilt and loneliness it causes.

Holmes, Richard, *Coleridge,* New York: Oxford University Press, 1982.

> Discusses the world of chaos and chance in *The Ancient Mariner.*

Purser, J. W. R., "Interpretation of *The Ancient Mariner,*" in *The Review of English Studies,* Vol. VII, No. 31, August 1957.

> Purser glosses the most important symbols in the poem in this readable article.

Radley, Virginia L., *Samuel Taylor Coleridge,* Twayne English Authors Series, New York: Twayne Publishers, 1966.

> A general introduction to Coleridge's major work, including *The Ancient Mariner.*

Twitchell, James, "The World above the Ancient Mariner," *Texas Studies of Literature and*

Language, Vol. 17, No. 1, Spring 1975.

> A study of the invisible world of spirits through which the Ancient Mariner sailed.

Whalley, George, "The Mariner and the Albatross," in *Twentieth Century Interpretations of "The Rime of the Ancient Mariner,"* Englewood Cliffs, NJ: Prentice Hall, Inc., 1969.

> Whalley discusses the symbolism of the Albatross and how the Mariner's experience mirrored Coleridge's own life.

htning Source UK Ltd.
ton Keynes UK
W022200200220
47UK00015BA/982

9 781375 397711